Q & A

Questions and Answers on the Nature and Existence of God

Nicholas Puleo

Contents

Intro

This is a true story. It is the report of a spiritual experience I had while studying, learning and asking questions about faith and religion. It was an experience that startled me and gave me a whole new perspective and understanding. It is the report of a Seeker who started from a very jaded view of faith and religion that even questioned whether God actually existed or not. As far as I know it is quite a unique and very different perspective. It is certainly like nothing I had ever seen or heard of before.

Having grown up unchurched in a house on a Catholic street in a Jewish town I had no idea what faith and religion were all about. As a child I noticed that most of my friends went to church or synagogue and asked my parents why we didn't go. I remember them saying that I could go if I wanted to. But since it seemed like just one more day of school, especially since my friends spoke of Sunday School, I passed.

Years later, having moved from the suburban Northeast to the rural South I experienced culture shock. It was not just over the slow pace of life, the oppressive heat, NASCAR, greasy fried food or the religion of college football. It was over actual religion, too. I was struck by the crowded church parking lots not only on Sunday mornings but Sunday evenings, Wednesday evenings and several other times per week. The first time I saw a crowded church parking lot on a Wednesday night I thought. "Oh, great, a basketball league! Probably CYO". It was not a basketball league.

I didn't think much of it until I realized how prevalent, or pervasive depending on your point of view, church participation actually was in my new hometown. I thought that organized religion was all there was to faith and religion. I never took it seriously and sometimes even thought it was kind of silly. I soon realized that the locals did not think it was at all silly. They took it quite seriously.

Most seemed like normal people and were quite sincere in their religious beliefs. And it disturbed me. Not because they believed in something I did not. This is America, you can believe whatever you want to, right? No, my uneasy feeling was secular, not at all religious in nature: somebody had to be wrong.

Either a large portion of the population wholeheartedly embraced something that was just not so, maybe a myth or even a fairy tale, or a large portion of the population was missing out on something most important. This wasn't a difference on the relative merits of country music vs. classic rock or which NASCAR team looked the best. This was a fundamental disagreement over nothing less than the very make-up of the universe itself, both the here and now and forevermore. I did not feel comfortable to be either in the company of a lot of delusional people, or just in case they were right, being left out of the Natural Order of things. The more I thought about it, the more concerned I became.

So I set out to do something about it. I investigated the question, became what some would call a "Seeker". I was close to, but not starting from absolute zero. Though I had no religious training or experience with going to church, I did have a vague idea that "something was out there". I had all the normal questions: Was Jesus *really* the Son of God? Did he *really* come back from the dead? Is the Bible meant to be taken literally or figuratively? Are heaven and hell for real? Why are some prayers answered and some not? Why do bad things happen to good people? And so on and so on.

I read books, attended a small, casual non-denominational Christian church, studied and asked a lot of questions. The teacher in adult Sunday school was a retired preacher. He was a brilliant man who not only knew all there was to know about Christianity and the Bible, but much more such as the origin of words from Greek and Aramaic that gave a different and more poignant insight into the standard doctrine most people are familiar with. He presented it in a mesmerizing fashion that captivated my attention. He was my mentor.

As I neared the end of my formal instruction from him, I still had several questions such as the ones mentioned above and more. He said that he had answered them in his classes and reviewed some, but if it still was not sinking in I should go home and say a simple prayer: He said to ask for the truth to be revealed to me. Though I still wasn't even sure what I was praying to, I prayed for guidance and said that prayer. Seek and ye shall find, right? And I did get answers.

A couple days after saying that prayer, a flood of ideas came into my mind. I wrote them down as fast as I could and the questions and answers in this book are the direct result.

The question and answer format in this book is just that, a format. While it could just as easily have been written as a straight narrative, or a story, or any other format, I did not consciously plan it or think "what should I write next?". This is just how it occurred to me. I even got a strong feeling that I was not the originator of these ideas, but that they were being related to me and I was just reporting on them.

So that is how I am relating this to you. Consider this the report of an earnest Seeker, and judge for yourself.

On the Nature and Existence of God

Q: Does God exist?
A: Yes, most definitely.

Q: Who, or should I say what, is He?
A: "Who" and "What" are both acceptable. God is the supreme power of all existence.

Q: Is God an entity? An individual? A person? A spirit?
A: An entity - yes - and individual in the sense that he is the singular pinnacle of all existence. Not a person and not a spirit, but closer to a spirit as you understand it. He is the Life Force in all things and is your Creator.

Q: So we have a beginning, then?
A: Yes, God created all that you see and are.

Q: All that we see around us literally, as in here on Earth, the stars in the sky, and more.
A: Much more. More than you can possibly imagine. All the grains of sand times all the grains of sand is inadequate to measure the scope of existence. It is indeed infinite.

Q: Infinite? There is no border to our universe? There's talk that the Hubble telescope can actually see to the end.
A: There is a border to your universe, and yes, that magnificent telescope can actually see close to the

end of it. Beyond that is infinitely more. Seeing only this universe is seeing practically nothing.

Q: So what is beyond our universe? Doesn't "universe" mean "everything"?
A: It may mean "everything" to you, but it isn't. "Existence" is a better name for "everything". Existence includes other universes, not unlike yours. As your solar system is to your galaxy, and your galaxy is to your universe, so are other universes to existence.

Q: Physical universes?
A: Physical universes and more.

Q: More? Like other dimensions?
A: "Dimensions" is a good term for it.

Q: And other times?
A: Time travels in one direction.

Q: You mean we can't go back?
A: You can't go back.

Q: I always thought that man was pretty creative and capable. It was thought the Earth could not be circumnavigated, but it was, we could not fly, but we did, etc. I always thought we would achieve the "impossibility" of time travel.
A: There is one significant difference and impassable roadblock: The earth is there to circumnavigate.

The air is there to fly in. The past is not "there" to go to. It does not exist anymore.

Q: What about the future?
A: Same thing. Can't go there because it doesn't exist yet. There's no place to go.

Q: Not even God?
A: Not even God.

Q: So God does not know what the future holds?
A: God knows what the future holds.

Q: How can he if he can't yet go there, or if it is not yet there for Him to look at? Does he script it?
A: God does not script it. He knows what will happen because he understands the interaction of all things and can predict what will happen with near certainty.

Q: Near certainty!? Not complete certainty?
A: God has set many things in motion that act independently of his direct intervention. He favors free will and independence in his creations.

Q: Like us?
A: Like you.

Q: So he can't control us?
A: Of course he can. He chooses not to.

Q: Never?
A: No, not "never". He intervenes.

Q: When does he intervene?
A: When it suits Him. Have you ever heard of The Grace
   of God? That is a polite way to say the whim of God.
   Sorry, but what may seem of utmost importance to
   you may not be so important to God. That he would
   ever pay attention to your specific situation is a
   most rare and precious, "gracious", act.

Q: Are we alone in the universe?
A: There is other "life" in the universe. Some you would
   recognize, much you would not. But mankind as
   such is quite unique. There are no others like you.
   You are among the more advanced creatures in
   existence as far as developing cultures and
   technology are concerned. You are practically if not
   literally alone.

Q: Will we meet other "advanced" creatures?
A: Not in your lifetime.

Q: Is the Big Bang Theory correct?
A: It is correct in describing how your portion of the
   universe was created.

Q: What do you mean?
A: I will put this in terms you may understand. God put
   a piece of matter, small in size but great in mass,
   and "exploded" it to cover the vast area of space

you call your universe. It was not a random scattering, but an intentional placement of the planets and stars.

Q: And comets and asteroids and everything else?
A: And comets and asteroids and everything else.

Q: According to our laws of physics, the transfer of energy in never 100%, something is always lost, so some think eventually the universe will degrade down to nothing. Will existence degrade down to nothing, to empty space?
A: No.

Q: Then our laws of physics are not valid.
A: They are valid.

Q: You just contradicted yourself.
A: No I didn't. You forgot already, your universe is not all there is to "existence". While your universe may degrade down to nothing, "implode" back upon itself by the force of gravity then continue crashing into itself until it eventually degrades down to cold, dark, dust, there is infinitely more outside your universe. The laws of physics you correctly apply to your universe do not necessarily apply to the rest of existence, and certainly not to God.

Q: Because God is supernatural?
A: No. Because God controls the laws of nature, not the other way around. God is not "supernatural"

anyway.

Q: *What?!*
A: God is not supernatural. Not in the sense he is
   separate or apart from nature. If you take
   supernatural to mean that you can not
   explain something according to your "laws of
   nature", that just means you can not explain it
   according to what you think the laws of nature are,
   not that that particular thing is beyond, or separate
   from nature. If you take "supernatural" to mean all
   powerful, then that does of course apply to God, but
   it is a poor use of the word. God is all powerful. God
   is the supreme power of existence. And that is a part
   of nature. God is the pinnacle of nature. While
   we're at it, actually nothing is supernatural.
   Everything is part of nature, by definition.
   Everything is a part of nature, nothing is separate
   from "Nature". It is meant to be that way.

Q: Does that mean that things reported to have been
   "supernatural", like angels, and demons, do not
   exist?
A: They do not exist per se.

Q: What in the world does that mean? Are people who
   have seen these things nuts?
A: Some are nuts. But these things have actually been
   seen.

Q: How can they have been seen if they do not exist?

Are they illusions? Dreams? Hallucinations? Aliens?
A: They are not aliens. We already covered that. Listen!
How can something be seen if that thing does not
really exist?

Q: A picture? A projection?
A: Ah, you're getting there. But a projection is merely
the *representation* of the thing in question. How can
you see the actual thing? Maybe this will help you:
it's temporary.

Q: An illusion? A hallucination?
A: OK. Enough twenty questions. It's a *manifestation*.

Q: A manifestation. So if you see a demon, for
example, it's not really a demon, just the
representation of one?
A: No! You're not paying attention. The manifestation
is real. So for the moment, the demon is real. But
only for the moment.

Q: I don't get it.
A: OK. When you were a kid, did you play with clay?

Q: I still play with clay. So what?
A: When you started out, what was it?

Q: A lump of clay?
A: Yes. And what did it become?

Q: Whatever I wanted it to become: a giraffe, a house,

a monkey. I wasn't very good at monkeys. And the necks on the giraffes always fell over. Again, so what?

A: And when you were done playing, what did you do with the clay?

Q: Smashed it into a ball. Why does that matter?

A: Think of what you just described: A lump of clay is transformed into a giraffe with a limp neck, then back into a lump of clay. Did the giraffe exist? Yes. Was it really a giraffe? No, it was clay.

Q: So God plays with clay?

A: Figuratively. The major difference is that his "giraffe" would come to life, making it an actual *manifestation*, whereas yours was technically just a *representation*.

Q: God can do that?

A: Of course.

Q: How?

A: God knows how to manipulate nature, matter and energy, into anything he chooses to. Even you can do that in your own relatively limited way.

Q: We can? What do you mean?

A: Here are two examples: You manipulate the force of gravity to light your house at night. It's called hydro-electric power. You take the force of falling water, gravity, and use it to generate electricity, which in turn you use to light your house. You also take electricity, "energy", and put it into an inert object, a battery, to store it. Well, God has infinitely more at his disposal than electricity. He has the actual Life Force, is the actual Life Force, which he can put into any object. The power and ability to do this is not totally unlike your ability to put electricity into a battery. The critical difference of course is His capability on an infinitely greater scale.

Q: That sounds too simple.
A: Again, complexity is not a required component of or a prerequisite for the truth.

Q: So God forms demons temporarily out of the stuff of the universe then unforms them.
A: God would not form a demon, he'd form an angel, but yes, he does.

Q: That sounds magical, supernatural. You said nothing is supernatural, didn't you?
A: Here is another illustration: Can you accept that God is more powerful than you? Do you believe that you in turn are more powerful than say, a worm? You are. A worm digs a tunnel in the dirt. Man builds the Lincoln Tunnel. Do you think the Lincoln Tunnel would seem miraculous or supernatural to the worm? Do you think the worm could even comprehend the Lincoln Tunnel? Are you so very proud of yourself just because you are more powerful than a worm? Are you so vain (and stupid

enough!) to think that nothing else could be that much more powerful than you? Why? Because you can't comprehend it? Don't even see it? Do you think the worm can comprehend you? Do you think he even sees you?! God is infinitely more powerful than you than you are of the worm. Trust me. He can transform anything he wants to into anything else he wants to. He can manifest the "stuff of the universe" into any form he chooses. It is not only not difficult, much less magical or supernatural, it is routine!

Q: Thank you.
A: You're welcome.

Q: Does God have a beginning?
A: There was a time when God did not yet exist.

Q: So he was born?
A: Not born, evolved.

Q: Evolved?
A: That's right.

Q: Um, I can't think of a proper question to follow that answer. Could you please explain it.
A: OK. Which came first, the chicken or the egg?

Q: Give me a break.
A: I'm not kidding. Which came first, the chicken or the egg?

Q: I have no idea.
A: It was the egg.

Q: The egg?
A: Yes, the egg.

Q: My hair is starting to hurt. Where are you going with
   this?
A: You asked me to explain where God came from, did
   he have a beginning.

Q: Yes, and I'm still waiting for your answer.
A: OK, here goes. You have heard people argue, in fact
   you've gotten involved in this argument yourself,
   about the question of did God create the universe
   or has it "always existed".

Q: Yes, So?
A: Well, what was your reasoning?

Q: I figured that the people who insist that the laws of
   nature must have been created intentionally
   because nature is so "orderly" were on shaky logical
   ground.
A: And why is that?

Q: Because if you insist on an explanation for the origin
   of the laws of nature just because they are
   "orderly" you must be consistent and also insist on
   an explanation for the origin of what created

those laws, which you would think would be that much more "orderly". You still haven't gotten to a starting point. Sooner or later you have to accept that something "always was". You can't keep insisting on origins or it never ends, or never begins. I mean you never get to an answer that way, right?

A: That's very good. Sooner or later you do have to accept that something "always was". Did God create nature and the rest of "existence", or was "existence", matter and energy, here first? Well, God was not here first by himself in a vast void. He did create much of "existence", including you and your universe, but he did not create the very first energy and matter. Energy and matter in their various and changing forms, have "always been". Then came God.

Q: You just pulled the rug out from under all we thought we knew of Creation. It is totally inconsistent with religious teaching. How can I possibly accept that?

A: I can see how you would see it as invalidating religious doctrine, especially Christian doctrine as told in Genesis. Do not despair. I will explain how it is compatible with religious beliefs including Christian doctrine, but we have more to cover first. We're not done with the evolution, the actual origin, of God.

Q: Tell me.

A: OK, The Laws of Nature and the "universe", actually

the more accurate term is "existence" remember,
have "always been". There has always been matter
and energy, interacting and interchangeable, even
as your understanding of physics describes with
some sophistication. Strict evolutionists, nonbelievers in God, describe life on earth as emerging
from the "primordial ooze" via a random interaction
of elements, forming carbon molecules, DNA, etc.
until it ignites into life. They are wrong. Life on earth
is far too complicated to have evolved at random
over time, even an incomprehensible amount of
time.

Q: Life on earth is too complicated to evolve at
   random? But God evolved? He is less complicated
   than life on earth? Oh, please help me with this. The
   Supreme Power of Existence is less complicated
   than we are? How is that possible?
A: Once again, why does something have to be
   complicated to be true? It does not. Yes, the
   fundamental make-up of God Almighty is less
   complicated than even you are.

Q: Please continue.
A: Even though God can not be explained in his infinite
   entirety to you, the essence of him actually can be.
   Think of him as pure energy. Pure positive energy.

Q: I will try to do that.
A: I am tempted to instruct you to not "try" to do that,
   but to just do it, but I will not for now. I know this

is difficult for you. Relax and let it come to you at your own pace. It is the Truth.

Q: Thank you for your patience. You did not complete the explanation of how God "evolved".

A: OK. "Existence" – energy and matter having "always been" – is the *original* "primordial ooze", a rambling, roiling, storm of interaction, totally random until things began to accumulate and form together. Like attracts like in nature. One particular accumulation of like material, both matter and energy but mostly energy grew and grew and added more and more unto itself, via gravity and other forces, until it became the largest accumulation of like material in existence. The accumulation of like things continued, being attracted more and more to more like things, and developed such an affinity for like things that the affinity became a tendency to gravitate to more like things, and the tendency to gravitate to more like things became an inclination to come upon even more like things, and the inclination grew so powerful that it became an actual seeking of like things, and the seeking became a compulsion to pursue like things, and the compulsion to pursue like things led to the differentiation between like and unlike things, and the differentiation between like and unlike things led to the recognition of like and unlike things, and the recognition of like and unlike things led to an awareness of the difference between like and unlike things, and that awareness led to consciousness. Consciousness led to sentience. Sentience led to observation, interest and curiosity and that set in motion a great accumulation of knowledge and experience. This accumulation took a vast amount of time and included the entire realm of existence. It included not only the observation of what was, but how it worked, how nature worked, how the forces of nature worked. The observation of how it worked led to the understanding of how to make it work, and the understanding of how to make it work led to the ability to master how it worked, and the accumulation of the knowledge of all things in existence and the mastery of how all things worked led to an all knowing and all powerful entity: God.

Q: All starting from the principle that like things attract like things in nature?
A: That was the beginning of it, yes. Attraction, then accumulation, affinity, tendency, inclination, seeking, compulsion, pursuit, differentiation, recognition, awareness, consciousness, sentience, curiosity, more accumulation and mastery.

Q: And what were those "like things" in the first place?
A: Mostly energy with some inert matter acting as a carrier for it, ending up being pure energy, the essence of God. What you are really asking me for is reassurance. Be reassured by knowing that it is so, which I will help you do. Try this (simple again) exercise to illustrate the principle: Look at the night

sky. Is it one vast homogeneous sight? Have like things been attracted to *un*like things forming a consistently bland, neutral landscape? No. The bright stars and dark void, "like things" unto themselves, are gathered together, distinctly separate. Do this exercise on a clear night. Contemplate it. Meditate and pray on the concept in the context of the above explanation. It will come to you.

Q: Can you give me more reassurance?

A: One more example: yourself. You have heard that man is created in God's image, or likeness. There is actually a semantic problem here, the word "image" being taken to mean actual looks: eyes, ears, nose, body and the rest of the form of a man. Physical appearance is irrelevant to this discussion. "Likeness" is the more accurate term. Man is "like" God in many ways. The evolution of God's own origin, his journey from the inert matter of existence to consciousness, self awareness and sentience, is the same journey an infant human takes in its own development. Look at the explanation again, the steps of having tendencies, inclinations, curiosity, observations, self awareness and the accumulation of knowledge and experiences. Are they not the same steps a human baby goes through? They are indeed. And why is that, do you suppose? Well, from where else would God draw ideas for his creations except his own knowledge and experience? He draws from his own experience just as you draw on your own. You go through similar steps of development because you are his creation, because you are created in his "likeness".

Q: Oh, my God.
A: Precisely.

On Religion and Spirituality

Q: One more time, please, the make-up of God is pure
   energy?
A: Pure positive energy.

Q: And His consciousness evolved from a vast
   accumulation and ultimately intentional pursuit of
   like things in nature?
A: Pursuit of like "things", like energy, knowledge,
   experiences, and more.

Q: Forgive me, but that sounds a bit like the old sci-fi
   story of the robot whose program becomes so
   sophisticated and he accumulates so much
   information he becomes sentient, doesn't it?
A: A crude analogy, but not totally inaccurate. That is
   how it happened.

Q: Is God a "He"?
A: Yes, God is our Father.

Q: What is the proper way to call his name?
A: "God" is fine. So is "Yahweh", "Jehovah", "Lord",
   "Father" or any one of many others. God is not too
   concerned with the name people call Him by, as
   long as it is reverent and respectful. One of the most
   accurate is "I Am" because God is the Life Force of
   existence itself, and the Life Force of existence
   itself is God.

Q: That sounds rather Zen-like. Is Zen Buddhism the
    true faith?
A: No. There is no one true faith on earth, though all
    of what you would call "major religions" have hit
    on at least some of the basic truths. But none of
    them have got it all right.

Q: My Christian friends are not going to be happy to
    hear that. What do I tell them?
A: Tell them not to worry.

Q: Not to worry! They're going to go berserk!
A: We'll address it later. Don't worry! Next question.

Q: Was Jesus the Son of God?
A: Yes, just as you and I are.

Q: What do you mean by that? Is there nothing special
    about Jesus?
A: I did not say there was nothing special about him. I
    just answered your question about whether he was
    the son of God or not. Yes, he is among the most
    "special". He was one of the few truly enlightened
    people ever to walk the earth. He had a very
    specific and important mission on earth, and he
    accomplished it magnificently.

Q: And what was that mission?
A: Pretty simple really. He told you to stop abusing
    each other and to love each other more, and that
    all were equally loved by God the Father. He also

wanted to help you by relieving you of the burden you had put upon yourselves with your sinfulness.

Q: Loving each other sounds like a pretty basic message. Why did it take the Son of God to deliver it?

A: It may sound basic to you, but it was not the way of the world 2000 years ago. Masters had their way with the enslaved, conquerors did as they pleased with the conquered. Rulers ruled absolutely and often cruelly. This was the culture of the time. Mankind was headed down the wrong path toward destruction. It was that serious.

Q: Why was Jesus' sacrifice necessary?

A: There are two sides to everything in nature: Equal and opposite reactions; Positive, negative, Good, evil, Light, dark; and on and on. To get something you have to give something. Call it a Law of Nature if you must call it something. Things must be earned. If something has been taken, it eventually must be paid for. Paid back or reconciled. Everything has a price and a value. Jesus' human life and the suffering he willingly endured were a great price to pay for a great debt. Someone else's debt. Your debt. This is what is meant by "Jesus died for your sins". He reconciled you with the Laws of Nature. With God. Self sacrifice for the good of others is the single most noble thing one can do.

Q: Did Jesus rise from the dead?

A: Not exactly.

Q: Help me here. How can you "not exactly" rise from
   the dead. It would seem that one either would, or
   would not.
A: The physical, human body of Jesus stayed dead.

Q: You just blew Christianity.
A: No, I didn't.

Q: Uh, yea you did. Isn't the core of Christianity belief
   in the Resurrection?
A: Yes.

Q: So if you don't have a Resurrection how can you
   have Christianity?
A: I didn't say there was no Resurrection.

Q: Yes you did, not two seconds ago! You said Jesus
   stayed dead. Now you're not only contradicting
   yourself you're denying your own words!
A: No, I'm not.

Q: The Disciples said Jesus appeared to them three
   days after he died. So did Mary Magdalene. Thomas
   put his finger in Jesus' wounds! Were they lying?
A: No.

Q: Will you please take a stand on this!? You're all over
   the place!
A: OK, when you finally die, that's it, your human life is

over.

Q: Even Jesus?
A: Yes, even Jesus.

Q: Then what happens?
A: Your physical body disintegrates and the essence of
you, your energy, joins the realm of God.

Q: "Essence" or "Energy", not soul? "Realm of God"?
Not heaven or hell?
A: You have no "soul", as such. There is no such place
as heaven or hell.

Q: Please explain.
A: Just as the essence of God is pure energy, so it is
with you, if on an infinitely lesser scale. While on
earth, the Life Force of God and your particular
thoughts, that is memories, personality, etc., are
contained in, reside in your mind in your physical
body. When your physical body finally dies, the Life
Force of God is removed and your Essence is
contained in, resides in a distinct place in God's
presence. You call it your "soul", but that is not
entirely accurate.

Q: How is that?
A: Being no longer self contained in a physical body, it
is not necessarily exclusively "you". Your
individuality remains, but your energy is also part of
a greater, well, collective consciousness if you

will. You are part of the sum total of existence.

Q: So does your individuality exist, or not?
A: Both. God allows your individuality to exist because
   he intended for you to be an individual, distinctly
   so on earth and as part of a collective consciousness
   thereafter. You were intended to experience
   your one lifetime for the sake of the experience
   itself and to gather knowledge. By the Grace of God,
   you may have more or less of an individual
   consciousness within his realm, but you are
   nevermore a completely separate "individual".

Q: And this "realm" is not a place? What is it, a "state"?
A: Yes. It is a "state". But you do continue to go places
   and have experiences.

Q: Real places?
A: Yes, real places.

Q: And what kind of experiences do you have?
A: Observations, learning, participation, discussions,
   things you would recognize as normal activities at
   first. They become more and more different as time
   goes by. Your consciousness as an individual is
   meant to continue developing, growing. Your
   experiences can be most enjoyable or most
   unenjoyable, depending on what you deserve and
   choose for yourself.

Q: Enjoyable or unenjoyable? Heavenly or hellish?

A: You could put it that way. Like I said, Heaven and hell do not literally exist as "places", but as experiences, well, yes, you could say they do.

Q: According to what we deserve or "choose"? We can choose?
A: You can choose to participate with the good, positive way of God, or not.

Q: Why would anyone choose anything but the good, positive way of God?
A: Why do people not choose the "right thing" on earth? It is one of the most astonishing and exasperating yet mysteriously endearing characteristics of the human condition, both on earth and later.

Q: And your status can change? Is your fate "eternal"?
A: It can change. You can develop, grow, enhance your status in the eyes of God and be rewarded accordingly.

Q: How are you rewarded?
A: By being allowed to experience more "enjoyable" things more "heavenly" things. Also by being allowed to operate more as an individual, and less as part of the collective consciousness.

Q: So we do not have to fear eternal banishment and torment in hell?
A: The hellish experience is something to be feared and

you can earn a sentence to it by your actions on earth.

On the Here and Now

Q: Will you help me with some more down to earth, here and now issues.
A: Sure.

Q: I am particularly interested in our country, the United States of America. Is it truly the greatest and most powerful nation on earth?
A: In secular and political terms, human terms, yes.

Q: Is that enough?
A: Enough for what?

Q: Enough to be considered truly great. Great in the eyes of God.
A: No human being, human endeavor, or human enterprise is what you mean by "*truly* great", that is, without fault or perfect in the eyes of God. Great, yes. Worthwhile? Yes. Noble? Yes, even appreciated. God appreciates the good things man does.

Q: Are we lacking in spiritual strength?
A: Do you really need me to answer that for you?

Q: I suppose not. We are a pretty sorry lot, aren't we?
A: Overall, yes, you are. There are some bright spots, but...

Q: Does that undermine our military and economic

might?

A: Undermine? Don't you mean invalidate it,
overshadow or trivialize it? Not in the eyes of God.
Your economy and military are of no consequence
to God. They are how you deal with each other, not
God.

Q: So why are we that way?

A: Pretty simple really. You are too impressed with
your culture, technology and creature comforts. It
wasn't always like that. In fact, it has only most
recently, the last 150 years or so, been like that.
More so and more so. Your "Founding Fathers"
sincerely intended to create "One nation under
God". They were spiritual men.

Q: So the way we deal with each other now does not
please God? We are not a righteous nation?

A: You are not a righteous nation. Recent events,
again, the last 150 years or so, have disappointed
God, but he knows you can and will do better. He is,
shall we say, optimistic.

Q: Is Democracy the best form of government? Is
Democracy in tune with the Laws of Nature?

A: Technically, you are a Republic, not a Democracy,
but we'll skip the civics lesson for now.
"Democracy", as you called it, is the best practical
form of government for human beings. The best
ideal form of government is a monarchy, for men,
"nature" or anything else.

That is how all of "existence" is run. I assure you,
God runs things as an absolute monarch. Not only
does He do what ever he chooses to do, he does not
consult anyone else, as a human monarch might. He
speaks, others do.

Q: No one chafes under that?
A: Those who directly receive the words of God are a
   very select very few. They are completely aware of
   their most privileged position. All in that circle know
   God does not need their input.

Q: Sounds like God has surrounded himself with a
   bunch of "yes" men.
A: I caution you: choose your words more carefully. I'll
   let that comment go for a moment and try to
   explain it to you: Is there any person you respect,
   think the world of and would be pleased to serve?
   Don't speak, I'll answer for you. Yes, there probably
   is. It is infinitely more so with God.

Q: Are you angry with me?
A: Yes.

Q: I'm sorry.
A: I accept your apology. Next question.

Q: If we are not an entirely "righteous" nation, we at
   least do sincerely attempt to do what's right. We
   do not start fights. We do not try to conquer the
   world though militarily we could probably pull it off.

We have no territorial ambitions. We protect
people from invaders and liberate them from
despotic and cruel rulers so they can be free. We
provide relief from natural disasters. Isn't that all
well and good?

A: To a point. You are also arrogant and presumptuous.
How can you be sure the objects of your
benevolence want your help? Desiring "freedom" is
what you want. Are you certain everyone else does?

Q: Most request our help, don't they?

A: Some do. Most do. But some of the "requests" for
help are orchestrated to give only the appearance
of sincerity. Your own agenda is really the driving
force. As for having no territorial ambitions, well,
that's not saying much for a country that already
spans from ocean to ocean with a desert to the
south and a frozen tundra to the north. Not exactly
noble. If Mexico was one big tropical paradise,
how long do you think it would be before it became
the 51st. state? And then there's the matter of
the original North American inhabitants. No
territorial ambitions, indeed. Easy to say when your
territorial ambitions have already been
accomplished.

Q: It's still pretty obvious most people prefer freedom
to subjugation, don't they?

A: Obvious to you. That's a value judgement. Your
values. Some places prefer homogeneity in their
culture and country. They want everyone to be all

of a particular religion or philosophy. That is not inherently wrong. Monarchy is the ideal form of government.

Q: Didn't you say Democracy was best for people?
A: It's the most practical. Monarchy is the ideal. More precisely, the ideal form of government is a benevolent monarchy, not just any monarchy. That's why it's God's way. Totally benevolent.

Q: Haven't we had some benevolent kings?
A: Yes, and Queens. But you have a very long list of very bad characters.

Q: Like who?
A: Read your history books.

Q: We are now involved in a war. We are killing people. God instructed us to not kill. Is there such a thing as a just war?
A: Yes.

Q: I don't recall the commandment saying "Thou shall not kill unless…" Isn't that a contradiction?
A: No.

Q: How is it OK to kill, them?
A: Another poor choice of words. It is not "OK", but it is permissible if there is absolutely no way to prevent others from killing. Preventing others from violating the commandment is as morally

acceptable as obeying the commandment yourself.

Q: So if someone threatens you, you can kill him before he kills you?

A: It requires more than just any threat. It certainly cannot be just a potential threat or you'd have to kill a lot of people. It has to be a real and imminent threat, not merely a potential threat. The one who threatens you endangers himself if he intends to kill you, makes that intention known and has the capability to kill you. Be most careful how you apply this. The prerequisites are narrow and specific, and the consequences for misapplying them most serious.

Q: So we are OK, morally, in our current war efforts?

A: You are. Your enemy has stated his intention to kill you, has made his intentions obvious and demonstrated his capability by actually killing some of you. There is no other way to prevent it. If you do not kill him where he is, he will come to you and kill you. As much as that saddens God, it is consistent with the intent of his commandment.

Q: "Intent of the commandment"? You sound like a lawyer.

A: If someone tries to deprive you of life, they run the risk of forfeiting their own opportunity. God wants you to experience your one lifetime on Earth. You are entitled to experience your one lifetime on Earth.

Epilog

And there the conversation ended as abruptly as it had started. It was not a conscious effort or at all intentional on my part. I did not sit there thinking "what should I write next?". The ideas just flowed effortlessly into my mind and then just stopped. I missed it. I tried to continue it, asked for it to continue, but it was over.

I felt comfortable, even gratified, with the whole experience. I felt that I had gained some new knowledge and reached a new understanding of things that had been troubling me. I liked the analogy of the tunnel digging worm being as unaware of the man made Lincoln Tunnel even if you put him right smack in it as we humans could be of an infinitely more vast state of existence, and even of God himself, no matter how intelligent or impressed with ourselves that we were.

I liked and was comfortable with the explanation of how God evolved from the existence of matter and energy because I could not reconcile God being both eternal and the creator of everything, of all of existence. That would mean that he sat in nothingness for an eternity before he did create everything in existence. Making the distinction between all of existence and our universe as being just a part of all existence reconciles with him creating our universe, this universe, and this Earth in the void that was here, validating rather than initially seeming to contradict our understanding of Creation.

After I read it, I realized that the answer stating that the resurrected Jesus was indeed seen, experienced and spoken to, but his body "stayed dead" was at first very troubling. I was concerned that it seemed to contradict a central tenet of Christianity, the Resurrection. But it actually did not and Christians need not worry, as stated. God's manifestation of a risen Jesus including the actual and original essence of him in a physical form recognized and accepted by the disciples as being the risen Jesus may not be the exact orthodox Christianity we have been taught, but it is a miraculous occurrence nonetheless and true to the promise of his Resurrection.

One of my favorite parts of all of this is the explanation of how we are made in the image of God, "where else would God draw ideas for his creations except his own knowledge and experience?" and the additional explanation that "image" does not necessarily mean a physical resemblance as much as the "likeness" of our essence, or character. The description and comparison of the growth and development of a human infant to that of God himself has a simple and gracious logic about it that I found to be reassuring and easy to comprehend and accept as the truth.

This led to an answer to of one of the biggest questions many people have that makes them question the existence of an omnipotent, benevolent God, "why do bad things happen to good people?". This answer incorporates three other answers given in this discussion. One is that God "does not script" our lives, "there are two sides to everything in nature" and the very last and most significant point made in all of this, "God wants you to experience your one lifetime on Earth. You are entitled to experience your one lifetime on Earth."

Think of how you treat your own children. Do you want them to experience and enjoy life? Do you nurture them? Help them? Protect them? Do bad things happen anyway? You could lock a toddler in his room, never let him out and he would never experience bee stings, scraped knees, poison ivy, maybe even a dog bite or a broken arm, but he would not experience all of the good things, either. On an infinitely grander scale, God sets us free, along with his guidance and protection, to have this amazing experience of our one life on Earth, both the good and the bad, just as our own parents do for us.

Still, some say, "Why?". Why does it have to be this way. Why can't an all knowing, all powerful benevolent God make this life a stroll in the park instead of allowing us to be inflicted by all of the trials and tribulations? If you believe this one life on Earth is it, it doesn't make any sense that he wouldn't, but in the context of this life being just one episode in an infinitely long (and unending?) experience, it makes perfect sense. We all know the old adage, life is a journey, not a destination.

In that context, it is important to remember that according to this discussion, God did not create the original laws of nature, he just learned to master them over eons to become the all knowing, all powerful pinnacle of nature. I suggest nonbelievers consider this: by definition, something in all of existence is the single greatest, most powerful entity, the pinnacle of it all, and it certainly is not man!

Which leads to one last observation. Our infant children cannot comprehend the details of all we are, what we know and what we can do, but they still learn to trust that we are here for them and to have faith in us. In a similar way, though we are intelligent creatures quite impressed with ourselves, we cannot comprehend all that God is, knows and does. All we can do is strive to understand what we are able to, have faith in God who knows all the rest and is infinitely more superior to us than we are of our own children, and I'm OK with that.

Again, I am grateful for having had this experience. I feel that I did indeed get answers to things that were troubling me and the answer to the original question my mentor said to pray for, to have the truth revealed to me. My intention in passing this along is not to advocate or argue for any particular or specific set of ideas, but just to be the messenger and the reporter. I am not the creator of these ideas.

Notes: